D0712928

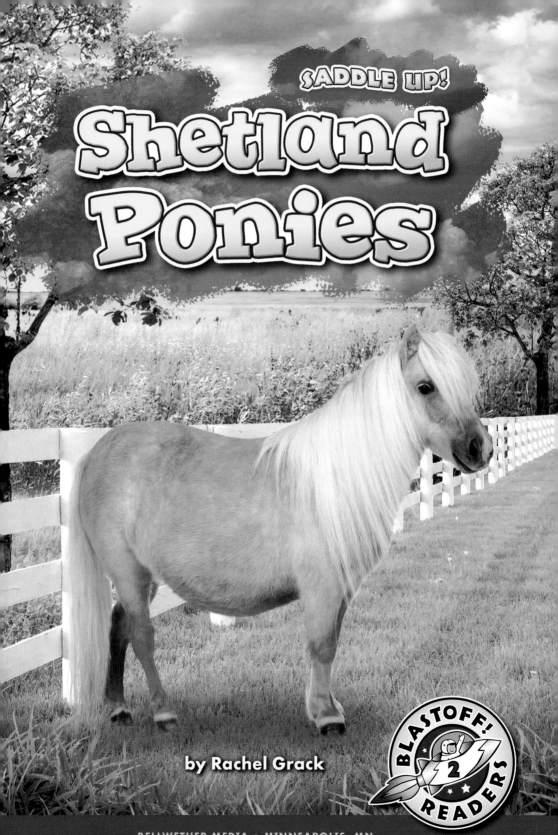

SADDLE UP!

Shetland Ponies

by Rachel Grack

BELLWETHER MEDIA · MINNEAPOLIS, MN

Blastoff! Readers are carefully developed by literacy experts to build reading stamina and move students toward fluency by combining standards-based content with developmentally appropriate text.

Level 1 provides the most support through repetition of high-frequency words, light text, predictable sentence patterns, and strong visual support.

Level 2 offers early readers a bit more challenge through varied sentences, increased text load, and text-supportive special features.

Level 3 advances early-fluent readers toward fluency through increased text load, less reliance on photos, advancing concepts, longer sentences, and more complex special features.

★ **Blastoff! Universe**

Reading Level

BLASTOFF! Beginners
Grade K

BLASTOFF! READERS
Grades 1–3

BLASTOFF! DISCOVERY
Grade 4

This edition first published in 2021 by Bellwether Media, Inc.

No part of this publication may be reproduced in whole or in part without written permission of the publisher. For information regarding permission, write to Bellwether Media, Inc., Attention: Permissions Department, 6012 Blue Circle Drive, Minnetonka, MN 55343.

Library of Congress Cataloging-in-Publication Data

Names: Koestler-Grack, Rachel A., 1973- author.
Title: Shetland ponies / by Rachel Grack.
Description: Minneapolis, MN : Bellwether Media, Inc., 2021. | Series: Blastoff! readers: saddle up! | Includes bibliographical references and index. | Audience: Ages 5-8 | Audience: Grades K-1 | Summary: "Relevant images match informative text in this introduction to Shetland ponies. Intended for students in kindergarten through third grade"– Provided by publisher.
Identifiers: LCCN 2020033239 (print) | LCCN 2020033240 (ebook) | ISBN 9781644874318 (library binding) | ISBN 9781648341083 (ebook)
Subjects: LCSH: Shetland pony–Juvenile literature.
Classification: LCC SF315.2.S5 K64 2021 (print) | LCC SF315.2.S5 (ebook) | DDC 636.1/6-dc23
LC record available at https://lccn.loc.gov/2020033239
LC ebook record available at https://lccn.loc.gov/2020033240

Editor: Elizabeth Neuenfeldt   Designer: Laura Sowers

Printed in the United States of America, North Mankato, MN.

Table of Contents

Small Horses

Shetland ponies are small, popular horses. Their small size makes them good **mounts** for kids.

But these cute horses offer much more than pony rides!

mount

Shetland ponies have
short legs and wide chests.
Their bodies are thick
and strong.

Many Shetlands weigh
around 450 pounds
(204 kilograms).

Most horses are measured in **hands**. Shetlands are measured in inches or centimeters.

They stand between 28 inches (71 centimeters) and 42 inches (107 centimeters) tall at the **withers**.

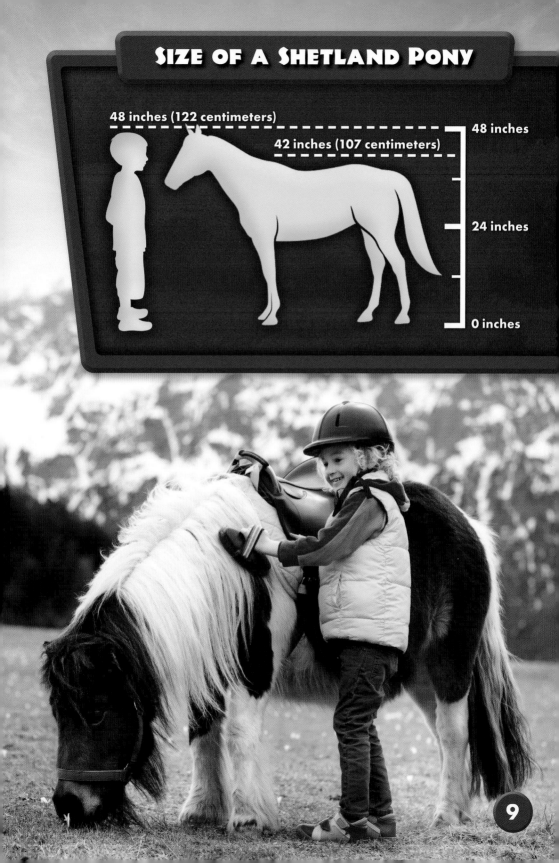

SIZE OF A SHETLAND PONY

48 inches (122 centimeters)

42 inches (107 centimeters)

48 inches

24 inches

0 inches

9

Shetlands can be almost any color.

gray

brown

tan

10

wiry
winter coats

Coats grow thick and **wiry** in winter. In summer, their coats feel smooth.

Shetland Pony Beginnings

Shetland ponies have lived on the Shetland Islands for thousands of years! They **thrive** in this cold **climate**.

In the 1840s, Shetlands worked as "pit ponies" in British **coal mines**.

Shetland Islands

Scotland

N
W ✦ E
S

Shetland Islands, Scotland

Shetlands first came to the United States around 1850. Americans **bred** them for riding.

SHETLAND PONY TIMELINE

OVER 2,000 YEARS AGO
Shetland ponies live on the Shetland Islands

1840s
Shetlands work in British coal mines

AROUND 1850
Shetlands first come to the U.S.

1888
The American Shetland Pony Club forms

In 1888, the American Shetland Pony Club formed.

Hard-working Pals

Shetland ponies
are hard workers.
They are also very strong.

These horses have been
used to pull carts and
plow fields.

Shetland pony race

Shetlands are smart and easy to train. They make great show horses for kids.

Shetlands shine in **driving** and **dressage**. Young riders race them, too!

two-wheeled cart

four-wheeled cart

Shetlands also like to have fun. Their friendly nature makes them good pets and **therapy animals**.

Shetland ponies are perfect pals for anyone!

Glossary

bred—mated with other horses to make horses with certain qualities

climate—the average weather conditions of a place

coal mines—places where coal is dug up from the earth; coal is a hard, black substance that is burned to create heat or power.

coats—the hair or fur covering some animals

dressage—a horse show event judged on movement, balance, and the ability to follow directions

driving—a horse show event in which horses pull wagons or carts

hands—the units used to measure the height of a horse; one hand is equal to 4 inches (10 centimeters).

mounts—horses used for riding

plow—to turn over soil by pulling a piece of farm machinery called a plow

therapy animals—animals that comfort people who are sick, hurt, or have a disability

thrive—to do very well

wiry—coarse and stiff

withers—the ridge between the shoulder bones of a horse

To Learn More

AT THE LIBRARY

Dell, Pamela. *Shetland Ponies*. New York, N.Y.: AV2 by Weigl, 2019.

Hansen, Grace. *Shetland Ponies*. Minneapolis, Minn.: Abdo Kids Jumbo, 2020.

Parise-Peterson, Amanda. *Shetland Ponies*. North Mankato, Minn.: Capstone Press, 2018.

ON THE WEB

FACTSURFER

Factsurfer.com gives you a safe, fun way to find more information.

1. Go to www.factsurfer.com.

2. Enter "Shetland ponies" into the search box and click 🔍.

3. Select your book cover to see a list of related content.

Index